CONTENTS

INTRODUCTION

I operate a small independent record label called Don Giovanni Records. When I first started releasing music I never had to worry about what the major labels were doing, or what any large company was doing for that matter. We were able to release physical records and CDs from bands in our music scene and have them listened to and distributed around the world through the help of local record stores and direct mail order. The label was able to sustainably grow and put out records, which received national attention from artists who were able to make a living off of their music.

As time went on, more and more companies from outside the independent community, and outside the music industry in general, started to show up, and would come to dictate the rules of the industry. First was Apple with the iTunes music store, which at the time was rather benign because we were able to offer an alternative for listeners who wanted MP3s by selling digital downloads directly off our website. It wasn't until streaming came along, led by Spotify, that things started to change in such a way that we could no longer operate sustainably without being involved in a system controlled by publicly traded multinational tech companies. At first we were able to resist on our own by simply not having our music on streaming services, but as their power grew it was clear that the only path to streaming music resistance would be from everyone, labels, artists, and listeners alike. I put together this guide to help explain the reasons for resistance and how best to accomplish it.

THE RISE OF STREAMING MUSIC

Streaming music allows you to play digital music directly from the internet rather than download a file that is stored on your device. In this sense, the data is continuously being received and played while never being stored anywhere. In the last decade music streaming grew nearly 30-fold to an 11.4 billion dollar industry with 341 million subscribers to digital service providers (DSP) like Apple Music and Spotify worldwide.[1] These tech companies are the winners in the new streaming landscape, and musicians and listeners are the losers despite the apparent convenience of the format.

It is not easy to stop streaming music, especially when some of the largest companies in the world have worked together to create an environment where it feels like the only reasonable option. From removing CD-drives in computers, to getting rid of CD players in cars, to stopping production of the classic iPod and similar devices, these

1 IFPI. "The Global Music Report." 2020.

companies have worked as quickly as possible to make even purchasing downloads of digital files feel obsolete.

As an artist and a label owner, I believe cultural resistance to streaming has to be driven by consumers, but should be led by artists and labels. I did not choose for streaming to make up 80% of the music industry in the U.S., nor do I choose America's domestic and foreign policy. Just as I am governed by the U.S., the music industry is currently governed by streaming. Neither leaving the country nor taking my music off streaming will solve the larger problem.

Rather, as a label owner and an artist I have an informed voice in the discussion about streaming, and implore all artists reading this to encourage your listeners not to stream your music. While my label's catalog is on streaming services, I do not personally stream music.

At the corporate level, the music industry has always grown profits by finding ways to get consumers to rebuy the same albums over and over again. Albums are continuously being reissued, remastered, repackaged, and collected into new definitive versions. This is because it costs far less to market a popular title with a built-in audience than it does to build an audience from scratch around a new artist or release.

In addition, with each new dominant format from vinyl to cassette, from CD to digital download, and from digital download to streaming, consumers are convinced they need to purge and rebuy their collection from scratch, often out of necessity as the devices used to play anything but the current format being pushed are quickly made obsolete. The CD format, for example, was developed by Sony and Phillips, two device makers. Apple and Microsoft developed digital download stores while they partnered with auto-makers to remove CD players from cars, and then when they wanted consumers to stream music, they stopped production on their own digital download playing devices.

Changes in format have always been motivated by profit, not quality or consumer experience, and so a paradigm like streaming, where consumers are forever paying for albums and never owning them, is extremely appealing to music industry executives. Listeners are now spending more than ever to listen to their music under the guise of spending less.

In the year 2000, when the buying of physical music was at its all-time peak, music buying consumers were spending an average of $64 a year on music,[2] only slightly

2 Pakman, David. "The Price of Music." 18 March, 2014, pakman.com/the-price-of-music-942cf2dcaa81.

more than half of what it costs for a year of an average streaming service at $9.99/month today. And yet, even with consumers paying more than ever to listen to music, less money is being paid to artists and songwriters.

The dismal payout to artists is well enough understood by most music listeners that people often ask what the most ethical way to stream is, or how the system can be fixed. But the answer is unfortunately not to stream music period, and that a system like this cannot be fixed. It would be like asking what the most environmentally sustainable way to produce Styrofoam is, when the answer is just not to use Styrofoam.

The problem is that while music streaming is ostensibly convenient, and thus appealing to listeners, we as a society pay a cultural, environmental, and economic price for that convenience that is so high it far outweighs the benefit of ease it provides.

Let's take a look at these costs:

THE ECONOMIC COST OF STREAMING MUSIC

They say streaming is a "don't own anything" paradigm, but it's actually a "you're always buying things" paradigm. Spotify uses the same predatory business model as a store like Rent-A-Center to ensure you are paying to rent something for life that you used to be able to just buy once for a much lower overall cost.

As a result, as mentioned earlier, music listeners spend nearly twice as much to stream music as they did at the peak of the physical music era ($120/year today compared to $64/year in 2000). Yet, when it comes to the artists, they now earn less money than ever before in the history of recorded music.

One cause of this disparity is how streaming services pay artists. None of them pay a true per-stream rate. Rather, they use a payment model called pro-rata.

In a pro-rata system, the total amount of money a service makes—from subscriptions and advertising—is divided by the total amount of all streams during that same period. This means artists get paid by the amount their songs are played relative to every other artist's songs on the streaming music service.

In other words, the value of a stream changes from month to month relative to the amount of songs streamed and the amount of paid users or ad revenue of a given service.

A pro-rata model is problematic for a number of reasons (the least of which being that it incentivizes artists to convince their fans to listen to no one else but them on the service). A pro-rata model denies listeners the ability to be socially or culturally responsible. For example, suppose you only want to support artists you align with and not financially support known abusers. In a pro-rata world, if you spend $9.99 a month and only listen to feminist artists like Bikini Kill, Bratmoble, and Team Dresch, then a significantly greater portion of your $9.99 goes to abusers like R Kelly and Chris Brown at the end of the month.

A pro-rata model also does not allow listeners to only support independent music the way they might in a physical or digital-download media paradigm.

In the CD/LP or digital-download era, the money you spent listening to an independent artist would only be split between the artist, their label, the store you purchased the album from, and the distributor who supplied the record to that store, if applicable. In the streaming era, most of the money you spend to listen to music goes to the top 1% of all artists on the service. This figure fluctuates from year to year, but anywhere between 80-90% of all the money coming in to streaming services is going to those top 1%.[3]

Streaming is a business model that only works for pop music.

In 2004, when the internet was still relatively young, Chris Anderson, editor-in-chief of *WIRED* magazine at the time, wrote a bestselling book called *The Long Tail* about the internet's ability to empower the niche, the alternative, and the small. Prior to the internet, retail was limited by costly physical space and had to only carry items that sold well and often. With near-infinite warehouse space, suddenly everything could be sold. This gave consumers more options and allowed small businesses to thrive. Further, the incremental sales of the niche products turned out to add up to as much as the whole of mainstream products at the top, providing an incentive for major online retail to carry niche items that didn't exist in the limited space of brick and mortar retail.

This power of the internet to unlock the potential of the niche was especially true in music retail where online music sellers could now carry a much wider variety of

3 Blake, Emily. "Data Shows 90 Percent of Streams Go to the Top 1 Percent of Artists." *Rolling Stone*, 9 September, 2020.

albums, and were selling more than ever. The millions of albums sold from millions of independent artists and labels were equivalent in dollars to the millions of albums sold from a small number of mainstream records each year, giving incentive for independent music to be sold and promoted like never before. During this period of time from the birth of the modern internet in 1999 to today, the independent sector of the music industry grew from 23% of the industry to 32.5%.[4]

In the pro-rata model of streaming music, however, independent records' relatively small numbers are pitted against their major label-controlled Top 40 counterparts in a zero-sum game. This gives the small labels and artists who sell slowly-but-surely no hope of ever competing fairly or making a living.

Artists Cannot Make a Living

At its core Spotify is a business model that is designed only to service hit songs, which in turn means it only serves the artists who make them: the top 1% . In fact, the top 10% of songs on streaming services account for 99% of all audio streams.

This makes it nearly impossible for non-hit-driven artists, or even hit-driven ones outside of the top 10%, to make a living.

Based on average rates[5], one million plays on Spotify will earn an artist between just $3,300 and $3,500 dollars. On YouTube it is even worse. If someone uploads your song to YouTube, that same million streams will generate less than $300 dollars. And yet, those YouTube plays account for 51% of all music streams, while accounting for only 6.4% of all streaming music revenue.

Prior to streaming music, it was possible for artists of all sizes and genres to make a living. Not just a comfortable living, but a living which afforded them time off from writing and performing so they could have a life outside of work, raise a family, or do other things that improve their mental and physical health. In the current paradigm however, streaming alone will not come close to paying 90% of artists minimum wage. And yet, streaming music accounted for nearly 80% of the industry's revenue in 2019.[6]

This puts 90% of artists in a position where the only way to make a living is to tour year round for their entire life, which takes an enormous toll on their mental health, physical health, and personal well-being.

---

4 MEI "World Report." 2000. | IFPI. "The Global Music Report." 2020.
5The Trichordist "2019-2020 Streaming Price Bible : YouTube is STILL The #1 Problem To Solve." 5 March, 2020, thetrichordist.com/category/royalty-rates-2
6 RIAA "Year-End 2019 RIAA Music Revenues Report." 2020.

THE CULTURAL COST OF STREAMING MUSIC

A streaming music paradigm doesn't just make it impossible for independent artists and labels to compete fairly with major labels or make a living, it is also a listening model that actively erases culture.

Suggestions, recommendations, and playlists—whether algorithmic or editorially programmed—serve to push listeners toward the pop hits that streaming platforms are built to promote.

For independent or alternative music listeners in any genre, before recommendation systems and streaming platforms, there were still sources for music discovery. These could have been record store owners, music magazines, college or non-commercial radio, blogs, message boards, artists thanked in other artists' liner notes, and others. Those listeners could spend one million hours interacting with any of those discovery models in 1999 and never be suggested Limp Bizkit, Shaggy, or any of their peers, despite them being among the most popular artists in the country at the time. And it was the very fact that there were spaces where these artists didn't reign supreme that allowed for a counterculture to exist and flourish.

Listeners today do not have to spend very long on streaming platforms before bumping into some of the largest pop artists in the world, regardless of what type of music they listen to. It is what these platforms are designed for.

Their hit-driven model strips music from its context entirely, turning all artists, no matter what their nature, into "greatest hits" artists, removing the work from its social and political context and recontextualizing it as something more marketable.

There is an even more direct cultural erasure enabled by the streaming platforms, like YouTube, that allow users to upload "their own" content.

For example, in 1972 a government employee named William DeVaughn saved up $900 to record a song he wrote called "Be Thankful For What You Got" at Sigma Sound Inc. in Philadelphia, PA, the kind of studio that advertised looking for talent in the back of music magazines. The song was a masterpiece and ended up selling over a million records, hitting #1 on the R&B Charts and #4 on the Hot 100. It has been covered by Massive Attack, sampled by N.W.A and Ice Cube, and referenced in songs by Parliament and Rihanna. And yet . . .

Today it lives on YouTube as "Diamond In the Back" by Curtis Mayfield, as uploaded by an unknown user. The version uploaded even employs the album cover of Curtis Mayfield's seminal self-titled 1970 album, despite the track not being on the record or being written by Curtis Mayfield. This video alone has 44 million listens, making it the most popular song attributed to Curtis Mayfield on all of YouTube and is included on official algorithmically generated Curtis Mayfield playlists. It is the second song that comes up when you search Mayfield's name, and there is another video of the same song with half a million views also misattributed to Mayfield.

Similarly, in 1998 Robbie Robertson drew from his Canadian Six Nations upbringing and his present interest in electronics, techno, and hip-hop to create *Contact From The Underworld Of Red Boy.* The album incorporated performances from Native singing groups like the Six Nations Women Singers, as well as a phone call from prison with activist Leonard Peltier. Robertson spoke in depth about the album and its recording process with David Fricke for a feature in the April issue of Rolling Stone that year, including about working with the Grammy Award winning duo Verdell Primeaux and Johnny Mike. The track Primeaux and Mike contributed to is called "Peyote Healing."

Today that recording lives on YouTube as "SPIRIT MEDICINE HEALING SONG - LAKOTA - (HQ HD)" with American Indian imagery, uploaded by an unknown user, and has 2.5 million views. Another video titled "Lakota Peyote ~ HEALING SONG ~" with similar imagery uploaded by a different unknown user has 2.7 million views. These versions are the first results that come with searches for Native American healing music and are among the top for Native American music in general.

This cultural erosion is enabled by a provision of the Digital Millennium Copyright Act (DMCA) called the Online Copyright Infringement Liability Limitation Act (OCILLA), most commonly referred to as the "Safe Harbor" Provision. The DMCA, which governs copyright on the internet in America today, and this provision, were both written in 1998.

For context, in 1998 only 26% of Americans even had access to the internet at home, compared to 82% today, with over 90% of the population using the internet.[7] The act was signed into law one year before Napster launched, six years before Facebook, seven years before YouTube and Reddit, eight before Twitter, and twelve years before Instagram. These corporations made vast fortunes primarily from the abuse

7 Pew Research Center. "World Wide Web Timeline." 11 March, 2014, www.pewresearch.org/internet/2014/03/11/world-wide-web-timeline/

and exploitation of the antiquated Safe Harbor Provision, and then they used those fortunes to lobby Congress to keep the act from ever being updated.

Simply put, the Safe Harbor Provision protects online service providers—such as search engines and social media platforms—from being liable when their users violate copyright law, so long as they agree to take down content when asked by the rights holder. With a staggering 500 hours of content being uploaded to YouTube alone every minute this puts an impossible burden on rights holders.[8] YouTube and other companies make billions exploiting this impossible burden that could never have been seen in 1998 when the laws were written. There will always be another unknown user to re-upload illegal content as soon as one version is taken down, while YouTube continues to serve ads and profit on this content the entire time, shielded by the Safe Harbor Provision.

In late 2013, YouTube automated the process of claiming content uploaded without permission to appease the music industry and other industries like film and television whose theft they were profiting from. Previously, those claims had to be made manually. YouTube has used this automation not to remove infringing content, or to stop it from being uploaded in the first place, but instead to continue profiting from illegally uploaded songs. Under this new model, they would make sure to pay the proper party.

This meant that for the example above, the money made from those 42 million streams of "Be Thankful For What You've Got" are going to William DeVaughn at least, instead of Curtis Mayfield or the unknown user who uploaded it. While this corrects the financial theft, the cultural theft and erasure is addressed nowhere, and this raises the necessary question of why, if YouTube can track the use of the song automatically for monetization, can they not simply block the content from being uploaded in the first place or immediately take it down? The answer is that they don't have to, and their parent company, Alphabet, would rather spend $21.7 million dollars lobbying to keep copyright law out of date so they can continue to profit off of the content.

The streaming providers that don't abuse Safe Harbor like Apple Music and Spotify aid in the erasure of culture in a different form.

8 Hale, James. "More Than 500 Hours Of Content Are Now Being Uploaded To YouTube Every Minute." 7 May, 2019, www.tubefilter.com/2019/05/07/number-hours-video-uploaded-to-youtube-per-minute/

Let's take a look at the same million-selling, influential William DeVaughn track on Spotify. It is not there. Possibly intentionally, possibly due to rights issues, but for whatever reason, the song, along with the 1974 album of the same name, is absent.

What is on the service instead is an album that never existed called *Be Thankful For What You Got*, with the cover art of DeVaughn's 1980 follow up album *Figures Can't Calculate The Love I Have For You* and a track-list containing songs from that album in a seemingly random order, book-ended by two equally out of place remixes of "Be Thankful For What You Got" by Philadelphia DJ David Todd. In addition to this album there is a 3:26 radio edit of the original 7+ minute version of "Be Thankful…" on a 5 track compilation EP called *70's Pop Gems*, and a similar compilation called *Can't Stop Dancing Volume 8* which also contains one of the David Todd remixes of the track.

Assuming that all of these parties have the rights to these songs, because Spotify does not verify this themselves, nothing on Spotify comes close to resembling what the original song sounds like. That in itself may not seem like much of a problem, similar to a great album going out of print and being unavailable in stores in its original form. The problems begin when Spotify editors and algorithms—out of ignorance, laziness, or sheer indifference—decide to use one of these "off" versions of the track on official playlists like *Soul Classics 1970–1975* or *The Black Power Mixtape 1967–1975*.

On those playlists and other official ones, like *Yacht Rock* and *Sweet Soul Chillout*, the original track is slowly erased from culture in favor of whatever versions were able to be licensed or uploaded to Spotify, as though there is no difference. As of this writing, various versions of the track other than the original have racked up almost 8 million plays. The original song itself, and the cultural context in which it was written, produced, and released, are lost.

Another example is in 1968, when The Holy Modal Rounders recorded "Bird Song," which ended up becoming a counter-culture classic after being used in an iconic scene in Easy Rider a year later. However, on Spotify, including on many official *Easy Rider* and *60s Counter-Culture* playlists, you will find a track from their relatively inessential 1978 album *Last Round* called "If You Want to Be a Bird, Wild Blue Yonder." That track is their most played song on Spotify as a result, and the first thing you will hear if you type in "Holy Modal Rounders."

For many punk and ska bands, their top track is a pop cover song done for a compilation or a 7" b-side, often as a throwaway, that hardly represents the band accurately. As you may imagine, covers of pop songs do quite well on streaming services. This recontextualizes artists and sometimes entire genres to be about pop song covers instead of the social and political environment the music originally came out of and was a part of.

For the band Pavement, their top song isn't from the album Rolling Stone named one of the top 500 albums of all time, but rather a random song from a CDEP that came out after the band broke up. The top song from Galaxie 500 is not one of their singles or even a song that represents their style as a band, but the song "Strange" which checks more boxes when it comes to algorithmic discovery. Both "Strange" and the Pavement b-side only rose to streaming prominence after adjustments were made to Spotify's autoplay feature and algorithms.

This re-invention of musical history is present all over Spotify and the other streaming services with arbitrary songs becoming massive hits for arbitrary reasons.

Let's be clear, this is not "musical discovery" as the streaming platforms may try to paint it. It is not a reflection of taste-making, but rather the previously described ignorance, laziness, or indifference among editors and playlist listeners fueling indifferent algorithms to create random hits completely unrelated to an artist's cultural relevance.

THE ENVIRONMENTAL COST OF STREAMING MUSIC

There is a widespread belief that streaming music is a green alternative to listening to physical formats, but this could not be further from the truth. Despite the lack of plastic or visible waste, streaming is actually a "disposable listen," the plastic fork or Styrofoam cup to physical media's metal or ceramic. Unlike a vinyl record or compact disc that is created once and can be listened to for a lifetime, each stream is created from scratch and transmitted to a device with every single listen.

But how can someone meaningfully compare plastic usage in a physical, media-based industry to energy usage in a streaming paradigm? One way to make meaningful comparisons is by looking at greenhouse gas emissions. According to research by Kyle Devine, if you translate the production of plastics and generation of electricity into greenhouse gas equivalents (GHGs), 140 million kilograms of GHGs were generated in 1977 during the peak of the vinyl era and 157 million in 2000 during the peak of the CD era.[9] In 2016—the most recent data available as of this writing—

9 Brennan, Matt, and Paul Archibald. "The Economic Cost of Recorded Music: Findings, Datasets, Sources, and

the streaming music industry was generating as much as 350 million kilograms of GHGs. The amount of music streamed has nearly tripled since 2016, so this number is likely significantly higher.

These emissions come primarily from data centers and server farms. Nathan Ensmenger refers to The Cloud as "a brilliantly wicked and misleading metaphor used to mask industrial waste and environmental impact in an idealized abstraction of something silent, floating, unobtrusive, and natural."[10] The truth about The Cloud and data centers, however, is that they consume enormous amounts of energy. If The Cloud were a nation it would be the 6th largest consumer of energy in the world, numbers which are expected to grow exponentially over the next decade.[11] Taken as a whole, the information and communications technology industries, which include data centers, mobile-phone networks, televisions, and personal digital devices, account for more than 2% of global emissions. This is roughly equivalent to the aviation industry, and steadily growing each year.[12]

In addition to the amount of waste created from data centers to create disposable listens, the devices used to stream music are just as disposable. The average time between phone upgrades is between just 16 and 33 months depending on brand and other factors.[13] According to the EPA less than 20 percent of old cell phones are recycled each year, and often end up in landfills; their composition includes toxic materials like cadmium, lead, and mercury, all of which can contaminate public food and water sources if not properly disposed of.[14]

Physical media on the other hand, especially CDs and vinyl records, are often fully reusable. Many record collections contain albums dating back to the 1960s and CDs dating back to the 1980s, that have been through multiple hands. Each time they change hands it is often mediated by a local record store or thrift store, which directly benefits a local community. These used media are rarely shipped around the country and generally stay within the community they came from via the local stores (with harder to find used media sold online being the exception).

In fact, a benefit of using a material like PVC plastic in vinyl production is its durability. Vinyl records can last forever. People will often pay more for older records than newer ones because they still sound so good. So while it's true that vinyl records

Methods." (2020).

10 Ensmenger, Nathan. "The Environmental History of Computing." *Technology and culture* 59.4, 2018: S7-S33.

11 Jones, Nicola. "How to Stop Data Centres from Gobbling up the World's Electricity." *Nature* 561.7722, 2018: 163-167.

12 Shehabi, Arman, et al. "United States Data Center Energy Usage Report." 2016.

13 The NPD Group, "The Average Upgrade Cycle of a Smartphone in the U.S. is 32 Months, According to NPD Connected Intelligence." 12 July, 2018, www.npd.com/wps/portal/npd/us/news/press-releases/2018/the-average-upgrade-cycle-of-a-smartphone-in-the-u-s--is-32-months---according-to-npd-connected-intelligence/

14 Wastecare Corporation. "Cell Phone Recycling." www.wastecare.com/Articles/Cell_Phone_Recycling.htm

are not recyclable or biodegradable, these same properties make vinyl records exceptionally durable and reusable.

This is not to say that physical media is great for the environment—it's not. Like most plastics, physical media is linked to the oil industry. A music industry that cared about sustainability would also work to avoid waste and overconsumption when it came to physical products.

Though not ideal, physical media worked. It sustained an entire industry of artists, record stores, and record labels, and the products themselves were relatively sustainable compared to the disposable digital alternatives that followed. The only reason CDs are so inconvenient is because the tech companies who owned the digital media devices and distribution platforms conspired to make them that way.

THERE ARE NO ALTERNATIVES TO "ALL YOU CAN EAT" STREAMING MODELS

The Big Three major labels—Universal, Sony, and Warner—have always had a "close" and controlling relationship with the infrastructure of the music industry, from chain retail to radio. However, there was also always room for an alternative, such as independent record stores, and non-commercial radio. This setup no longer holds true when it comes to streaming platforms like Spotify. They rely on an enormous user base, complicated software that's expensive to develop, and massive server space. This situation forces mainstream artists and record labels to compete against alternative ones within the confines of these platforms. But the platforms are also owned in part by, or have favorable deals in place with, the Big Three. This relationship becomes problematic because truly independent artists and labels will never be able to fairly compete with the Big Three on platforms that the Big Three control.

For a reasonable amount of money, anyone can open an independent brick and mortar record store, or sell digital downloads directly to customers. But the costs of starting an interactive streaming service or social network are astronomical, requiring the kind of partnerships and financing that would no longer make a platform independent.

We are shifting toward a system that forces artists, labels, and consumers to accept these platforms, tying themselves to their boom-bust cycle, to their consolidation, and to whatever arrangements they have to offer.

Maybe it's time we cleared away The Cloud? Broadband is getting faster and hard drives get larger and cheaper. Music doesn't take up a lot of space. Unlike something like a film, music is meant to be portable and experienced over and over again in different locations. It seems like the main benefit of pushing music into The Cloud and streaming delivery mechanisms is to quietly consolidate control into the hands of a smaller and smaller group of players.

It is time to stop asking how we can make streaming work, and start asking: why are we pursuing streaming in the first place?

Maybe what scared the major music and technology companies about the digital music environment wasn't piracy, but that it threatened to actually democratize music, turning it into a space where big and small could compete with each other more fairly. The push to on-demand full-catalog streaming as the primary form of music consumption undoes that level playing field, shifting power back into the hands of a small group of major labels and tech companies.

We need a future where alternative voices are not forced to exist *within* the corporate-controlled streaming music infrastructure, but can stand as a true alternative to them.

A CULTURAL SHIFT AWAY FROM STREAMING

While many are quick to point out that now that "all you can eat" streaming is here that there is no way to get people to go back to an older model, society has proven time and time again that this is not the case. This is not asking us to take a step backward. Rather, streaming must be understood as a mis-step in the wrong direction, like Styrofoam or DDT. We must get back on the right track, as soon as possible, so we can continue to move forward.

There are also many who point out streaming is just like radio, which is also free. First it is important to recall the environmental and cultural impacts of streaming described earlier. If streaming is simply providing a similar service to you as your radio, then you are creating massive amounts of unnecessary environmental waste and greenhouse gas emissions by choosing streaming. The cultural erasure described earlier does not occur on radio to the extent it does on streaming services. It is also important to note that radio is regulated and streaming services are not. There is no FCC governing streaming services, payola is perfectly legal there, for example.

The streaming era will end when there is a cultural shift against it. It will always be an easier, cheaper option, just as Styrofoam was for various disposable products in the past. The move against Styrofoam toward more environmentally sustainable alternatives was a cultural one. Similar cultural moves have been made regarding tobacco, road safety, clean energy, and plastic drinking straws.

There is a precedent for this in the music industry as well.

Streaming music has not taken off in Japan as they have different cultural norms toward music. In Japan, streaming makes up less than 20% of the market and CDs make up almost 70% of the market.[15]

Vinyl and cassette tapes have resurged around the world in recent years as cultural norms shifted around their usage. As few as ten years ago it was very difficult to find vinyl record players, and only a select number of stores carried vinyl. There were only a few vinyl pressing plants and manufacturers in the country. But as a cultural shift happened among consumers, pressing plants opened, manufacturers started making turntables again, and all record stores started carrying vinyl.

A move away from streaming and back into physical media or even digital files will be no different. There will still be a place for streaming, just like there will be for Styrofoam plates and plastic forks. Office parties, child's birthday parties, and other occasions may still call for the use of disposable materials, and there will be cases when streaming is the best option too. But it should never be the only option. It needs to be a "sometimes" alternative for times when listening to music more responsibly is too difficult.

In a world where streaming is the exception rather than the norm, the planet will be cleaner, culture will be better preserved, artists will be better sustained, and you will still get to enjoy everything that is so special about music. The streaming era is over, if you want it.

15 Pastukhov, Dmitry. "Music Market Focus: Japan." 2019.

TAKE ACTION TODAY!

Stream Music as Little as Possible

Think of streaming audio the way you would think about a Styrofoam plate or a plastic fork. There are contexts in which they are the best option, but should not be the norm.

Cancel Your Streaming Subscription

Streaming platforms' main source of profit is from paid user subscriptions. As they grow in size, they use their power to make it more difficult to listen to music in any way other than streaming. Cancel your subscription today and consider spending the $10 a month building up a library of digital audio downloads, CDs, LPs, or Cassettes that will last you a lifetime.

As an Artist or a Label, Advocate for Your Audience Not to Stream Your Music

Educate your listeners on the unsustainable position it puts you in when they stream your work instead of downloading it or buying a physical version. Real change will only come from listeners cancelling subscriptions and bringing their business to places that sell downloads or physical media.